These good dogs and their owners are speaking up for a worthy cause: royalties, contributors' fees, and a portion of the publisher's profits have all been donated to The Company of Animals Fund, which offers grants to agencies that care for the welfare of animals. Previous grants have provided veterinary services and found homes for stray or abused animals, developed humane education programs, and helped care for animals in the homes of the elderly and the ill. For more information about the fund, write to Michael J. Rosen in care of Harcourt Brace & Company in San Diego.

Art Center College of Design
Library
1700 Lida Street
Pasadena, Calif. 91103

741.6420922
S741
1993

SPEAK!

CHILDREN'S BOOK ILLUSTRATORS BRAG ABOUT THEIR DOGS

Edited by Michael J. Rosen

HARCOURT BRACE & COMPANY
SAN DIEGO NEW YORK LONDON

Compilation and additional text copyright © 1993 by Michael J. Rosen
"Buddy-boy" copyright © 1993 by Petra Mathers
"Okie" copyright © 1993 by Lane Smith
"Rosie" copyright © 1993 by Natalie Babbitt
"Tiny" copyright © 1993 by William Joyce
"Blacky" copyright © 1993 by Karen Barbour
"Olive" copyright © 1993 by J. Otto Seibold
"Jipper" copyright © 1993 by Marc Rosenthal
"Frank's Dog" copyright © 1993 by Lucy Cousins
"Patsy" copyright © 1993 by Stan Olson
"Scat" copyright © 1993 by Tim Bowers
"Heidi" copyright © 1993 by Lisa Campbell Ernst
"Tipper" copyright © 1993 by Peter Hannan
"Newman" copyright © 1993 by Ted Rand
"Frodo" copyright © 1993 by Richard Jesse Watson
"Hero" copyright © 1993 by Judy Pedersen
"Gee Gee" copyright © 1993 by Carolyn Gowdy
"Dog" copyright © 1993 by Seymour Chwast
"Clinton" copyright © 1993 by James Ransome
"Beezo" copyright © 1993 by Michael Paraskevas
"Sally" copyright © 1993 by Wendell Minor
"Liza" copyright © 1993 by Fred Marcellino
"Crystal" copyright © 1993 by Merle Nacht
"Dog House" copyright © 1993 by Douglas Florian
"Arambarri" copyright © 1993 by Alexandra Day
"Taffy" copyright © 1993 by Paul Meisel
"Buick" copyright © 1993 by Tim Lewis
"Tip" copyright © 1993 by Rodger Wilson
"Prince" copyright © 1993 by Thomas Wharton
"Charlotte & Emilio" copyright © 1993 by Barbara Westman
"Beau" copyright © 1993 by Peter Catalanotto
"Muffin" copyright © 1993 by Alice Provensen
"Mr. S." copyright © 1993 by Betsy Everitt
"Sheila" copyright © 1993 by Robert Andrew Parker
"Buster & Ben" copyright © 1993 by Trina Schart Hyman
"Bongo" copyright © 1993 by Arthur Yorinks
"Rocco" copyright © 1993 by Gary Baseman
"Bruno" copyright © 1993 by Victoria Chess
"Jojo" copyright © 1993 by Steven Guarnaccia
"Buster" copyright © 1993 by Thomas B. Allen
"Pinkerton" copyright © 1993 by Steven Kellogg
"Roosevelt" copyright © 1993 by Barry Moser
"D-Dog" copyright © 1993 by Elizabeth Sayles
"Duchess" copyright © 1993 by Aminah Brenda Lynn Robinson

All rights reserved. No part of this publication may be reproduced or transmitted in any form or by any means, electronic or mechanical, including photocopy, recording, or any information storage and retrieval system, without permission in writing from the publisher.

Requests for permission to make copies of any part of the work should be mailed to:
Permissions Department,
Harcourt Brace & Company, 8th Floor,
Orlando, Florida 32887.

Library of Congress Cataloging-in-Publication Data
Speak!: children's book illustrators brag about their dogs/edited by Michael J. Rosen.
p. cm.
Summary: A collection of illustrated anecdotes about dogs by forty-three children's book illustrators includes those by Seymour Chwast, Alice Provensen, and Trina Schart Hyman.
ISBN 0-15-277848-9
1. Dogs—United States—Anecdotes—Juvenile literature.
2. Dogs—United States—Pictorial works—Juvenile literature.
3. Illustrators—United States—Anecdotes—Juvenile literature.
4. Dog owners—United States—Anecdotes—Juvenile literature.
[1. Dogs.] I. Rosen, Michael J., 1954– . II. Title: Children's book illustrators brag about their dogs.
SF426.5.S66 1993
818'.540208036—dc20 92-30325

Designed by Molly Leach, New York, New York
Cover photograph of Harry the Dalmation by Dennis Mosner
Printed and bound by Tien Wah Press, Singapore
First edition
B C D E

REINFORCED TRADE BINDING
PRINTED IN SINGAPORE

[c o n

ributors]

[introduction]

I like to brag about my dogs.

Most people I meet like to brag about their dogs. Most dogs I meet, on the other hand, don't brag about their people. Oh, a dog might feel that the person on the other end of the leash can do some pretty swell tricks, but dogs just aren't braggers—they're believers. A dog's whole day is spent believing that its people are the very best on earth.

But people are braggers. Over and over, we tend to brag about good things, perhaps because we just can't believe we deserve them. And dogs—well, dogs may be the best good thing that ever happened to people.

On these pages, some favorite illustrators brag, in pictures and stories, about their dogs. But instead of the flattery and the long parade of doggie virtues you might expect, what you'll find are scenes from the oldest and richest companionship we humans have enjoyed with another creature. When we SPEAK! up about our dogs, we not only celebrate our unbelievably wonderful, 12,000-year history with dogs, we also join the world of dogdom—a world where repetition is happiness, a world of playfulness, unbounded feelings, instant forgiveness, constant affection, and a devotion with a pull that rivals gravity.

Surely, before you meet the other prized companions in this book, I should brag a little about the two retrievers that share my home.

My golden retriever, Paris, is gold only in color, though he acts as if he's worth his weight in genuine gold. (At eighty pounds, that would be close to half a million dollars.) Paris isn't a show dog, but if there were an award for Best of Show-Off, he'd be champion. His special talent is, of course, retrieving, but Paris will try anything to get your attention. Want proof? Invite us over. He will bring out the biggest stuffed animal from your closet, operate any squeaking, musical pop-up toy lying about, and volunteer such tricks as imitating an upright groundhog—his signal for more chest-scratching—and dusting the coffee table with his tail. (Be ready to retrieve anything a tail might whisk away.)

Madison, my yellow Labrador retriever, isn't a show-off. He isn't really yellow, either, though once, when we raced through a field of dandelions, his legs were stained a brilliant yellow. His coat is more like the color of a sugar cookie; his eyes would be the raisins. Madison isn't much of a retriever, for that matter, and he'd never go exploring through your house. Maybe he had enough exploring when he was a stray puppy. Now, as if to thank me for giving him a home, Madison is my constant companion. His serious, self-appointed job is: stay close. True, at times he stays a little too close: under the wheels of my office chair or curled up in the garden bed where I've been trying to dig.

One last story I have to tell is that both my dogs were once lost. When Paris and Madison slipped away from my parents, who were caring for them, I was thousands of miles away, reading from another book dedicated to helping animals. Madison wasn't even wearing a collar. It lay behind a chair at my parents' house because Paris had invented a new trick: tugging off his pal's collar and parading it around like a trophy. But after hours of searching by a network of caring people, after a TV station broadcast a holiday snapshot of my dogs unwrapping presents with my nephews, after endless visits to concerned shelters, and after a call from the manager of the Waffle House, who, at last, spotted the dogs, we found them: fifteen miles, two freeways, a creek, and almost three days away from where they'd begun, huddled together beneath an ice-coated evergreen in a shopping mall parking lot.

That story had a lucky ending. But luck doesn't always favor dogs. Dogs have given up many of their natural ways to cross the boundary between our species and join our families; for this, each dog deserves lifelong care and protection. Yet stories are told every hour of people failing their dogs. That's why SPEAK! has another purpose: it is one in a series of books where I've asked writers and artists to donate work, so that when you buy a copy, part of your money can directly help lost, abused, and homeless animals. Grants from SPEAK! will provide spaying and neutering assistance, veterinary care, humane education, and support for people struggling to keep the dogs they love.

And finally, SPEAK! not only tells stories, it invites them. As you read this book, I hope you'll remember stories about your own family dog. I'd be delighted if you would SPEAK!, too, and send me a little bragging about your favorite dog. (Write to me in care of Harcourt Brace & Company, Children's Books, 1250 Sixth Avenue, San Diego, CA 92101.) In the meantime, enjoy these forty-three do-gooders' tales of their own good dogs. You have lots of treats ahead.

MICHAEL J. ROSEN

PETRA MATHERS

[buddy-boy]

I COME from Bide-a-Wee.
I have no pedigree.
My past's a mystery.

I've been with them for ten years now.

They don't know my age. I keep 'em guessing.

I don't hear so good anymore.

I don't see so good anymore.

I snore and sneeze,

scratch and shed.

I go clickety-click up and down the hall at five A.M.

I love to eat. There is never enough.

I put up with them.
They put up with me.
We are a family.

[o k i e]

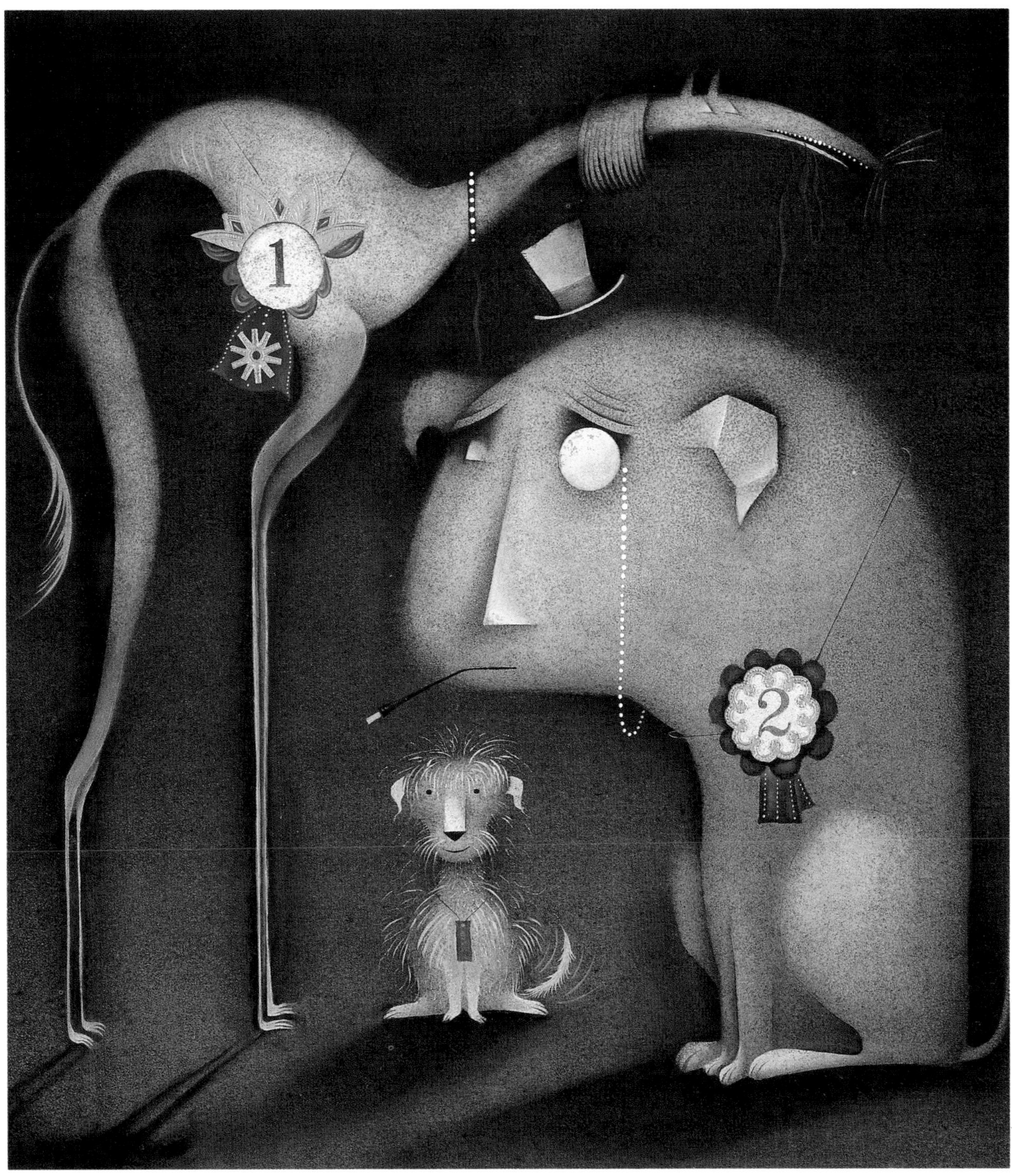

WHEN I WAS in second grade, my school had a dog show. Some fancy-schmancy hairy thing that had been all dolled up at the groomer took the second-place ribbon. First place went to an out-of-town ringer named Zinfandel. No surprise there: Zinfandel had graduated from dog school and could carry her own leash.

The real surprise came when my dog, a mutt named Okie, was awarded her own ribbon.

Later, in the car, my mom gave Okie a pat and told her how proud we were. I held up the ribbon and we read it together: "Participation."

LANE SMITH

BOWWOW, yellow dog,
Have you any hair?
Yes, marry, have I,
Lots to spare.

Plenty for the furniture,
Plenty for the floor,
But none for the vacuum
That lives behind the door.

Hark, hark! the dogs do bark!
Mailmen are coming through:
Some with bills, and some with frills,
And some with postage due.

Old Father Hubbard
Went to the cupboard
To give his poor dog a bone;
But when he got there
The cupboard was bare
So she had an ice-cream cone.

[r o s i e]

One, two,
Sticks to chew;
Three, four,
Claw the door;
Five, six,
Fleas and ticks;
Seven, eight,
Clean the plate;
Nine, ten,
Sleep again.

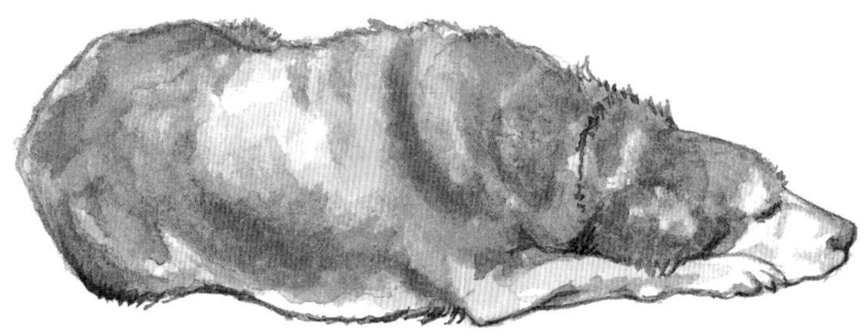

4

IN EVERYONE'S growing up there should be an all-American, true-blue, one-of-the-family, bowwow wonder dog.

Mine was Tiny, a black dachshund with regal bearing and the heart of a lion. No intruder—human, animal, or insect—was safe when Tiny patrolled our (really his) domain.

Tiny committed the bravest act I have ever seen. He grabbed a wasps' nest in his teeth, tore it from the ceiling of his modest doggy home, and despite the frenzied stinging of the wasps, dragged it out and tossed it defiantly into a puddle by the hydrangeas. I'd like to see a human—any human—do the same.

It's little surprise that in my boyhood dreams he was Tiny—ace of dogs, weary adventurer of the animal underworld; Tiny—space dog of the stratosphere; or, simplest and best, Tiny—my pal, my pet, my dog.

[tiny]

WILLIAM JOYCE

[b l a c k y]

MR. FEWT PAID thousands of dollars for a dog from France. He brought him up to his big estate and named him Grandchamp du Château d'Ayen d'Escargot. The dog wouldn't sit and he wouldn't lie down. He dug up Mr. Fewt's Charles de Gaulle roses and he never came when he was called. "Grandchamp du Château d'Ayen d'Escargot, you are a no-good dog!" Mr. Fewt yelled. "I will not tolerate this impossible behavior."

Grandchamp du Château d'Ayen d'Escargot ran away. That's when I met him. I took him home and named him Blacky.

KAREN BARBOUR

[olive]

SOMETIMES when we wake up, Olive is already talking about how, maybe, the hot-dog man will give Mr. Lunch and her some hot-dog buns.

[jipper]

7

MARC ROSENTHAL

MY FATHER-IN-LAW Jack's dog story #6: "Unfortunately, the screen door stood between Jipper and the attacking june bug."

FRANK IS a baby.
Frank lives in my house.
Sometimes he sits on my back.

Sometimes he pulls my tail.

But I like Frank. I always sit next to him at teatime.

PATSY HAS never shown much interest in finding birds. It could be that she realizes I don't care much about finding birds either and figures that if all I want to do is spend the day walking around in fields she would be happy to tag along and keep me company.

[patsy]

A DISTANT rumble . . . Scat's black-and-white ears cocked into listening position. I tensed. We both knew something was coming. An old green station wagon turned the corner onto our street. Scat's head lowered. He gave a quiet growl and we watched the long green car approach. Suddenly Scat exploded into action.

I'd seen it a hundred times before—Scat chased every truck, car, school bus, and bicycle that happened to stray onto Windmere Drive. But never, before now, while I was holding the other end of his leash!

TIM BOWERS

LISA CAMPBELL ERNST

HEIDI WAS A dog with an appetite, always searching for dropped crackers, forgotten cookies, stray Cheerios. She often saved some for later, hiding tidbits in nooks and crannies around the house. My father was rather unhappy the day he found a cold pancake tucked in his favorite chair.

One Easter, my brother, sister, and I woke to find baskets packed with Easter Bunny loot: eggs (dyed, chocolate, and marshmallow), bunnies, and jelly beans. But we had to dress and rush to church.

When we returned, our baskets were a dismal sight. Only the paper grass remained. Bits of eggshell and shreds of colored foil were scattered everywhere. And Heidi? She sat nearby looking sheepish.

Then the real Easter egg hunt began: behind couches, under rugs, in Heidi's bed. Of course, nothing we found was still edible. But it didn't matter. Heidi made the best Easter Bunny ever.

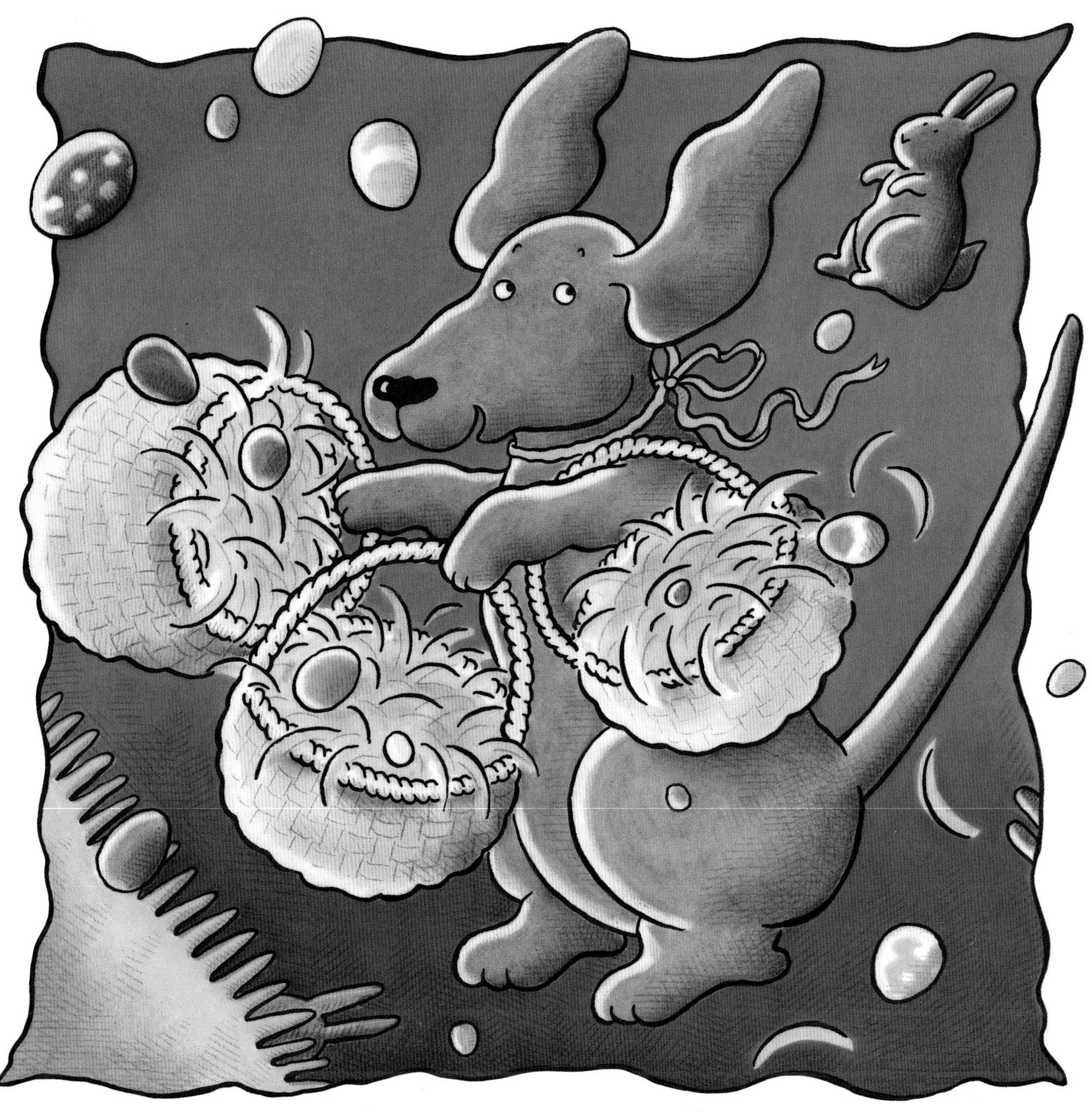

[heidi]

[tipper]

HE HAD LOST a leg to a Chevy, but that didn't slow Tipper at all. He could almost fly, whipping his tail around like a propeller, and he could outrun any dog. He was a celebrity. "Whoa!" kids would say, "Tipper is your dog?"

One hot day my mother saw him lying on the lawn, barking at nothing. "Woof! Woof! Woof!" "Tipper, come!" "Woof! Woof!" "TIPPER!" "Woof! Woof!" "NOW!"

At last he jumped to his feet, but something was wrong. Ordinarily a three-legged wonder, now he limped awkwardly toward the house. When he staggered up the porch steps, my mother saw the problem. His right front paw was caught in his collar. He had run to her on two legs. Two left legs.

"I'm sorry," said my mother as she untangled him. "Woof, woof!" said Tipper. Then he whirled his propeller and took off across the lawn.

PETER HANNAN

[newman]

TED RAND

I MET NEWMAN and his master last year when I was illustrating a picture book about companion dogs. This golden retriever spends his days and nights with a boy who has muscular dystrophy.

I've owned a variety of dogs, but no dog has touched me quite like Newman. He wears a pack when he's on duty at school and his eyes and behavior are all business. He can obey more than eighty commands. But Newman has a split personality. Home from school, his pack removed, Newman is another dog, a great galumphing golden. He sheds his responsibilities and he's ready to play.

HE STARTED OUT as a Pasadena Dog Pound puppy with big paws. One day a guy from Germany told me, "*Das ist und Leonberger.*" I looked it up: *Lionhound.* "Wow. What do they eat if they can't get lions?" I wondered.

RICHARD JESSE WATSON

Everything else. Frodo ate insects and rabbits and he actually enjoyed eating bricks. He tried to eat lawn furniture, faucets, our garage door, three metal buckets, a goat, a bolt of lightning, two animal shelters, and nearly the entire state of Kansas.

Some days he'd sneak off to the back door of the neighborhood bakery. "Oh, it's poor hungry Butch; toss him some croissants and doughnuts." Next stop, the butcher. "Here, Hank . . ." Meat scraps. The cafe: "Here, Pooch." The burger joint: "Here, Wally." At the Kentucky Fried Chicken drive-thru, he put his paws up on the ledge: "It's Buster!" Extra-crispy out the window.

He's in heaven now. Hunting lions. Or tossing them doughnuts from his very own bakery.

[frodo]

[h e r o]

JUDY PEDERSEN

ON NOVEMBER 20, 1968, our dog Hero, awakened by a dream, bolted from his warm sanctuary of a den and flew off into the night. We never saw him again, but every night we waited for him to return.

MY SISTER AND I would look forward to each week's episode of "Lassie." Lassie was a collie renowned for rescuing people, animals, and so on, every week.

As the theme music played and the credits rolled out, our favorite dog sat and gazed out of the television at my sister and me. We would kneel to kiss her face, sometimes with such passion that we left our lip prints on the screen.

One day, our parents took us to the local dog shelter. We all hoped we might find our own dog there, one who needed some love.

Right away, my sister and I were drawn to a tiny dachshund in the corner of the yard.

Her sensitive brown eyes seemed as deep as Lassie's. She was shaking from head to tail. We sensed she needed rescuing—not by Lassie, but by us.

Settled in at home, our new dog, Gee Gee, my sister, and I gathered in front of the television, week after week, to watch Lassie perform another rescue.

SEYMOUR CHWAST

HAVING A DOG around (like having a beautiful car in the driveway) makes me feel like a responsible, important squire—I realize that anything is possible and I'm ready for adventure. I empathize with the sadness people feel when they lose a dog. A poet once observed:

"The gods weep at the death of the dog . . .
The dog, that when he looked at them thus,
asked: Where are we going?"

[clinton]

AWAKE . . . a wag . . . a walk?
spotted sleuth: scratching, sniffing
squirrels beware!
inside, outside, beside,
overjoyed to be underfoot
football, Frisbee, felines
belly-up begging
for beef-basted biscuits
polka-dotted, liver-spotted
rollicking, frolicking, romping, rolling
sighing, stretching, spotted spiral

JAMES RANSOME

[b e e z o]

THIS IS MY friend Beezo.
Every year she attends the horse show.
The Hampton Classic's main event,
Under the big striped grand prix tent,
Believe me, wouldn't be the same,
Without this Jack Russell,
And Beezo's her name.

GROWING UP in the Midwest without a dog is like being a farmer without a tractor. From the time I was born until the time I left Illinois for college, there was always a dog in my life. Ranger, Bucky, Laddie, Sally, Checker, Brownie, Timmy, Sunny, and Fluff—I remember every one of them with great affection.

But Sally was special. Springer spaniels, by their very nature, are always a bit flaky, but Sally was just plain crazy. She was most unpredictable and undisciplined when the moon came into its fullest phase. Month after month, the full moon beckoned to Sally, urging her to run away and chase moon shadows.

Eventually I realized that our lovable Sally was more predictable than any of us imagined—we could always predict she'd be at her looniest when the moon was full.

[s a l l y]

[l i z a]

WAS IT A misguided rescue attempt? Or was *I* retrieved instead of a stick? Either way, on one summer afternoon many years ago, Liza the Labrador proved herself a true friend, or one dumb retriever, or both.

FRED MARCELLINO

DAVE AND RUTH ANN, my neighbors, got a new dachshund they named Crystal. Afternoons around four o'clock, when I'm often hurrying to meet a deadline, Crystal would start barking. Her little yipping barks made me tense; the more it happened, the worse I felt. I tensed up just thinking about the barking.

One day I bumped into Ruth Ann walking Crystal. While we were talking I became aware of a pleasant warmth on my right foot. Crystal was sitting on it. She stayed there—quietly and calmly, even with dignity—as Ruth Ann and I chatted. In that moment, I discovered there is no way not to love a dog that sits on your foot. Never again did Crystal's barking bother me.

A few weeks ago Ruth Ann and Dave moved away and new owners moved in. No barking, so far.

[crystal]

23 [dog house]

MY BEDROOM'S full of bulldogs
My bath with basset hounds.
A Saint Bernard romps in my yard
While Great Danes roam the grounds.
My pinschers pinch my pillows
Chihuahuas climb my chairs
And sixteen Irish setters sit
Serene along the stairs.
A dachshund dashes 'cross my desk
A beagle's on my bed.
A Pekingese and toy Maltese
Are sleeping on my head.
I've poodles by the oodles
And Scotties by the score.
My pointers point out paintings
While bloodhounds block the door.
They eat from ample platters
And drink from giant vats.
But something here
Is very queer—
I dream all night of cats.

DOUGLAS FLORIAN

WHEN MY BACK was injured, I had to rest it by spending many weeks in bed. My husband and children, though they came often to see me, sometimes became absorbed in activities of their own. I was frequently alone—except for Arambarri, my rottweiler. He was my constant companion, lying usually between the bed and the door, so that no one could get to me without his knowing.

One afternoon I was very thirsty, and all my banging and shouting failed to get anyone's attention. So I wrote a note, called Arambarri, and told him to take it to someone downstairs.

A few minutes later he reappeared, carrying a basket containing a bottle of water. After that I used him as my delivery dog all the time. He could carry anything we could fit into his basket: books, a thermos, flowers, pillows, food (which he never touched), and whatever else I needed. He seemed to enjoy his job, and I was grateful for the help and delighted by the grave devotion of the messenger.

[arambarri]

PAUL MEISEL

MOST OF MY childhood was spent with Taffy, a beautiful and sweet-natured rough collie. As Taffy grew older, she began to have trouble with her legs, a condition that is common with her breed. Going down the back steps to the yard, Taffy would bounce on her front legs, unable to use her rear legs for anything more than balance. Dad built a ramp so Taffy could avoid the difficult stairs altogether.

When winter came, Taffy's legs were stiffer and movement was even more difficult. On one particularly snowy day, Taffy asked to go outside and didn't return as usual. My father went looking for her and found her stuck in the snow, unable to move. She was waiting patiently for someone to come get her, and there she stood, as dignified and regal as ever. That's how I'll always remember her.

[t a f f y]

[buick]

I HAVE FRIENDS in northern California who like to drive through the countryside. Their dog, Buick, enjoys these rides, too—especially when he sees a cow. If anyone in the car says "cow," Buick tears around to each window until he locates the cow. To avoid being trampled by Buick, we had to make a car rule: never say the word—spell it out—c-o-w.

[t i p]

OUR BORDER COLLIE was named Tip because he had a white tip on his tail. Tip came into the family when I was turning eight, before I realized the difference between a working dog and a pet. But Tip knew and somehow he was able to be both. Tip had duties around the barns. I wanted to help, too (being very grown-up, I thought), and Tip was as tolerant of me as could be.

One day we were bringing the milk cows into the barn from the fields. I walked in front of a cow, and she charged me. So Tip leapt in front of the cow to protect me—he jumped right on the cow's head. The cow bucked, jumped, and threw Tip off. By then I was out of danger, so Tip got up and continued the task at hand: moving the rest of the cattle into the barn.

After the cows were in, Tip became a pet again, as though switching back and forth were the most natural thing in the world.

[p r i n c e]

MY DAD FOUND Prince at one of those general stores where you could buy anything from a carton of worms to a wedding dress.

From the beginning, Prince and I shared everything—including his dog biscuits, which I thought tasted better than my mother's bridge mix.

Prince liked music and sang along enthusiastically when anyone—especially my mother—would sing his favorite, "Indian Love Song." He loved everything about my mother except her high-heeled shoes. When she dressed up, he would bark at her feet, and occasionally one of her shoes would turn up in a neighbor's flower bed.

Prince lived to be an old dog. I was in college when my mother called to tell me they'd found him lying in a pasture as if he'd gone to sleep.

That night I went out and bought a box of dog biscuits.

THOMAS WHARTON

[charlotte & emilio]

ONE DAY Arthur and I went to get a puppy. When two puppies tumbled forward, I said, "Oh, let's get both!" We decided to name our new springer spaniels Charlotte and Emilio, almost like the Brontë sisters.

One night in our tiny house on Long Island, Arthur and I were dancing to some schmaltzy radio music. Emilio, who loves music, danced with us, and Charlotte soon joined in.

When we go out now, we always make sure the radio is on. We like to think that, instead of snoozing, Charlotte and Emilio dance the night away.

BARBARA WESTMAN

GET DOWN! Every morning the same. Beau would come loping into my bedroom, roused by the sun, crashing the door into the wall, vaulting onto the bed, barking and howling.

Get down!

My yelling did some good. Beau still hates being the only one awake in the morning, but now he doesn't make a sound. He thinks he's being good.

He pushes the door with his nose. Quiet as a tail wag, he crosses my room and flops his head on the edge of my bed. And he breathes his dog breath on my face until I wake up. You really can't yell at a dog who believes he's being good.

[b e a u]

[muffin]

MUFFIN IS part Hungarian puli and part French poodle. She was born in America and is a good citizen and a fine friend.

But the problem with Muffin is that she grows too much hair. And she won't let you give her a haircut.

In spring, when the days get warm, Muffin sheds most of her long black winter overcoat, but she never, *never* loses one hair on her head. You can't help laughing at the way she looks. She is sometimes called Fat Head or Bubble Head.

Her nicest nickname, however, is Beloved Black Peony; for whatever her appearance, Muffin is a much-loved dog.

Here is Muffin communing with the flowers in the garden.

ALICE PROVENSEN

[mr. s.]

OF COURSE, Mr. S. has been gone for a while, and his bone-balancing act was, perhaps, not quite as dramatic as I recall. (My mother has tried to convince me that the bone "balanced" rather unexcitingly on his stomach.) But in my little-girl memories, Mr. S. is always amazing.

BETSY EVERITT

[s h e i l a]

WE HAD A dog we named Sheila, a stray that appeared at our house one Sunday morning. I think someone had let her out of a car. She was old and very calm. I imagined she had been a dog that would carry her master's *Daily News* in her mouth.

She stayed with us for a while and then wandered off to the neighbors'. They named her Daisy.

After she left us I dreamed she jumped out of a plane over Ireland, landing softly on the green hills. Then I made a series of drawings about Sheila hovering over all sorts of places. This is one.

ROBERT ANDREW PARKER

BUSTER AND BEN live in the country, and they never have to be tied up or walked at the end of a leash. They are free to roam the fields and woods, to hunt skunks and frogs and woodchucks, to just sleep on the porch, or to go visit the neighbors. They know better than to chase the cows and the sheep, but they will sometimes chase the occasional jogger or pickup truck, just for fun.

Buster and Ben are best friends. In their hearts they are brothers, although, in fact, Buster is a purebred Doberman pinscher and Ben is a mutt. Buster is a gentle soul—kinda goofy, with a perpetual air of bewilderment. What he lacks in brain power, however, he makes up for in good manners, courage, and sensitivity. Ben is a shrewd customer—fast, smart, jaunty, and stubborn. He's the brains of the team, and Buster is the brawn.

Each day is a new adventure, and they share it side by side.

[buster & ben]

[bongo]

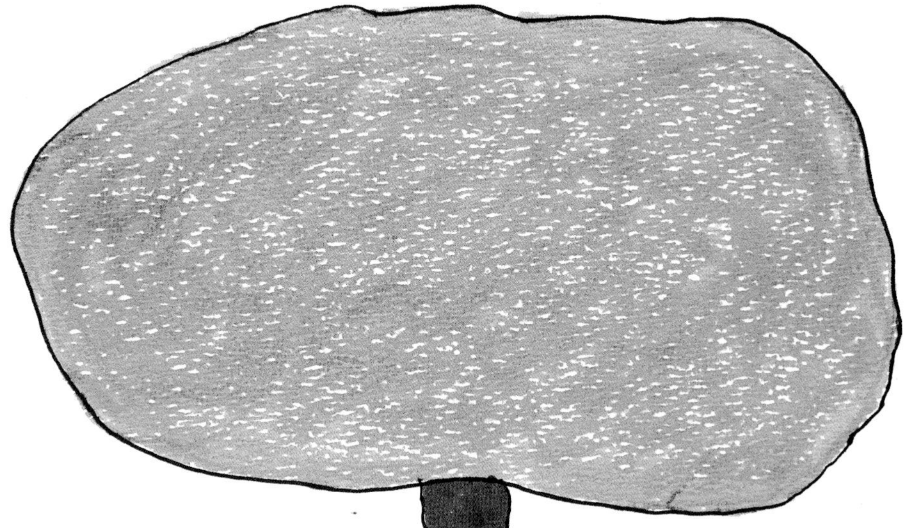

THIS REALLY happened.

It was spring. Syd, our golden retriever/German shepherd mix, was sick. She had a tumor on her leg. We tried to comfort her by wrapping a warm cloth around the lump. Syd's friend Bongo, a Border collie, sat next to her in the yard to keep her company. Maybe they thought about how they used to steal bologna together. They always did everything together.

One day, Syd, who loved to eat, couldn't. We took her to the vet and, sadly, she died. We cried and cried. Bongo wanted to cry, too. Back at the house I gave Bongo a Milk Bone to try and cheer her up. She wouldn't take it. I broke it in half and she ate half. Then she took the second half and scratched the back door to go outside. She walked to the spot where we had sat with Syd and began to dig a hole. Gently she placed the broken biscuit in the hole and, with her nose, covered it with fresh dirt.

There Bongo sat, one last time, remembering Syd and saying good-bye to her old friend.

ARTHUR YORINKS

FROM THE VERY beginning, Rocco wasn't an ordinary canine. He was extremely loyal, but that didn't distinguish him from other pooches. When he first arrived, he followed me everywhere. He loved attention. He would always come up to guests, entertain them, and ask to be petted.

I never needed to teach him to fetch, either. He had a little windup toy that he loved to carry in his mouth and drop in my lap or by my feet. His bottom wiggling in the air signaled me to wind and throw. We'd play the game ten or twenty times in a row.

He also wasn't afraid of dogs twice or three times his size. But that didn't really make him stand out from other dogs, either. I guess you can say what made Rocco unique was that he was born a kitten.

[rocco]

VICTORIA CHESS

WHENEVER BRUNO takes a trip around the neighborhood, he never fails to bring us a present. These are some of the nice things he's come home with: a bunch of bananas, a dead woodchuck, a red ball with blue stars, some dead squirrels, a chicken (not dead), two beer bottles, a deer antler, a can of evaporated milk, a very large zucchini squash, and a bottle of suntan lotion.

Best of all was Mrs. Baker's purse—it had eighty dollars and fifteen credit cards inside.

[bruno]

[jojo]

JOJO WAS my uncle Sam's dachshund. Uncle Sam and Aunt Jean lived in Vermont in a house that faced the road in front. Their backyard went straight back, and then tumbled down a wooded mountain.

Jojo was a porcupine chaser. She was so low slung and snaky that she seemed to be able to turn two corners at once. In the morning, she'd scramble out the back door, legs a blur and toenails scratching the flag-stones. She'd head out for the woods, where she'd stay for half a day. By afternoon, she'd come back with quills sticking out of her jowls in all directions. She'd gaze dolefully at Uncle Sam and quietly suffer his firm but gentle hand as he plucked spines from her muzzle.

But a porcupine, standing its ground, eye to eye with Jojo, must have seemed a delicious challenge.

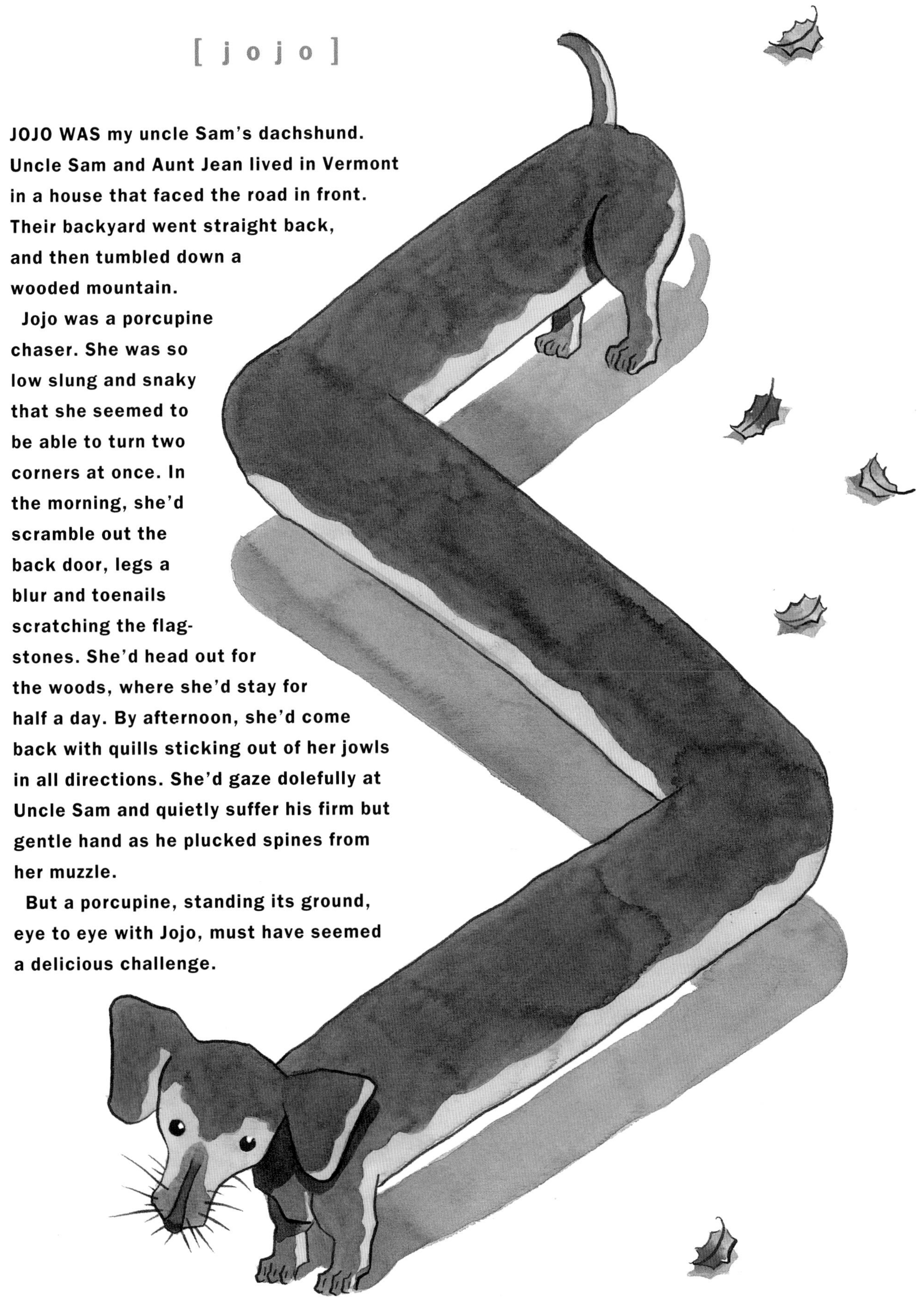

[buster]

BUSTER WAS lost for three days in Tulsa. A man saw him running along an exit ramp, stopped his truck, and chased him down. The man and his family took care of him and answered my ad in the newspaper.

I drove down to Tulsa the following weekend to pick up Buster. Boy, was he one happy little Yorkie.

HE WAS NINE weeks old and a pudgy piglet when he shuffled into our lives. When he was four months old, his hind legs grew longer, and suddenly he could LEAP like a kangaroo. He loved to bound into my studio to snatch erasers. Pinkerton thrived on his diet of erasers, and five months later he resembled a holstein bull.

On our woodland rambles, he enjoyed chewing down trees. I wondered if he would grow up to be a giant beaver or a piebald version of Babe, the blue ox.

At one year old, and still growing, it was obvious that he was becoming a GREAT DANEOSAURUS.

BARRY MOSER

FRANKLIN D. ROOSEVELT, my rottweiler, looks like he could eat little children for breakfast, but he's really a gentle Goliath who's afraid of gerbils. Rosie runs faster asleep than awake, and intellectually he's not much swifter, carrying an IQ that I figure hovers somewhere near 10 on bright, sunny days.

Although his intellectual gain has been minimal over the years, his heart has multiplied many times. Though he growls at his four-legged housemates when they approach his bones or toys, my granddaughters, Isabelle and Emmaline, easily retrieve objects from his huge mouth. They use his tailless haunch as a sliding board, push him out of the way with impunity and, God bless them, they read to him—in that wonderful blab-blab that toddlers make up as they turn pages—all snuggled up against his chest. Rosie listens. Head up. Eyes shut. I think he understands their language.

[r o o s e v e l t]

[d - d o g]

THIS IS D-Dog. D-Dog is short for dirty dog. We called him that because he was always dirty, even after a bath.

He used to visit the butcher down the block and beg for bones. Then D-Dog would bring the bones home and bury them in my bed. But there were limits: I always made him take them out before I went to sleep.

[duchess]

DUCHESS WAS just a dog dog. She was given to me by my father, who dearly loved animals; before his passing, he passed this new life on to me.

On April 8, 1983, Duchess gave birth to nine puppies. The first puppy arrived at nine-thirty that evening. I sat up, drawing sketches and asking myself how this miracle can happen. Duchess whispered to each new puppy as she cleaned it. Eight were mostly brown with speckles like flowers. One was all tan. The very last puppy was born nearly twelve hours after the first, at nine the next morning.

At the end of the exhausting experience, the new mother listened to the timeless songs of her family, hearing the echoes of the songs she and her brothers and sisters used to sing when they were growing up in a world full of sunshine, kindness, and love, a world full of people who cared deeply for each of them.